Ready, Set, Know Your Bible!

Kayla Coons

Ready, Set, Know Your Bible!

Inspiring Devotions for Kids

BARBOUR kidz
A Division of Barbour Publishing

Print ISBN 978-1-63609-262-1

Published by Barbour Publishing, Inc., 1810 Barbour Drive, Uhrichsville, Ohio 44683, www.barbourbooks.com

Our mission is to inspire the world with the life-changing message of the Bible.

Printed in China.

001095 0422 DS

Contents

On your mark. . .

get set. . .go!

You usually hear those words at the start of a race. They are words that are full of energy and excitement. This book will help you to get ready, get set, and *know your Bible*! You can be energized and excited to learn more about God, the world He made, His Son Jesus Christ, and the salvation He offers everyone if they'll only ask.

God is your heavenly Father. He knows and loves you so much better than anyone else ever could. Getting to know Him through His Word, the Bible, is the best thing you could ever do. So get ready, get set, and know your Bible—from Genesis to Revelation—and keep on learning, every day of your life!

Genesis

Ready. . .

In the beginning God made from nothing the heavens and the earth.

GENESIS 1:1

Set. . .

Animals, people, sky, and earth—
God's the one who gave them birth.

Know Your Bible!

Have you ever wondered where everything came from? Oh, you know that *you* came from your parents, and they came from their parents, and their parents came from their parents. . . .

But who were the very first parents? Where did *they* come from? Who made their food and their water and the trees they used to build their house?

Why is the sun in the sky? Where did the moon and the stars come from? How can we possibly know these things?

There is an answer to all these questions. . .it's God! And the place to find that answer is the Bible, which is God's Word!

The Bible is one big book made up of 66 smaller "books"—and Genesis is the book at the very beginning. (Did you know the word *Genesis* means "beginning"?) When you read Genesis, you'll learn that God made everything. . .animals, people, sky, and earth. He also made—and loves—*you*!

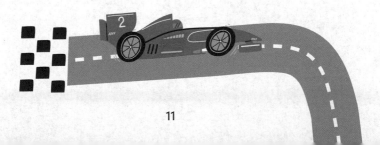

Exodus

Ready. . .

Then the Lord said to Moses, "Go to Pharaoh and say to him, 'The Lord says this: "Let My people go, so they may worship Me."'"

EXODUS 8:1

Set. . .

For God to set His people free
He would even part the sea!

Know Your Bible!

In Genesis, God chose Abraham as His special friend. Abraham's family became a large group of people called "Israel." For many years, they lived happily in Egypt.

But a new leader of Egypt was selfish and mean. Pharaoh made life hard for the Israelites. They cried out to God for help. And He listened!

God sent Moses to tell Pharaoh to let the people leave. Pharaoh kept saying *"No!"* So God punished Egypt with terrible plagues. Bugs and frogs covered the land. People and animals got sick. Many in Egypt died.

Pharaoh finally let God's people go. But as they reached the Red Sea, crazy Pharaoh changed his mind! He sent his army to stop the Israelites.

That's when God did something really amazing. He split the waters, making a dry path through the sea. The people walked across safely. When Egypt's soldiers followed, the water crashed back over them.

God always hears, loves, and protects His own people.

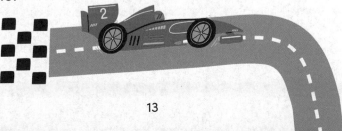

Leviticus

Ready. . .

I am the Lord your God. So set yourselves apart, and be holy. For I am holy.

LEVITICUS 11:44

Set. . .

Sinful people need to do exactly what God wants them to.

Know Your Bible!

Churches have people who help others know God better. Pastors preach from the Bible. Sunday school workers teach important lessons. Elders and deacons serve people in many ways.

Long ago, when Moses led Israel, "church workers" were called Levites. They were the family of a man named Levi. And the Bible's book of Leviticus tells how they should help the people to know and please God.

God is perfect in every way. He is "holy," which means He is set apart from everything else. Humans are *not* perfect. Genesis shows how Adam and Eve disobeyed God. That was sin, and sin keeps people away from our perfect God.

But He wants people to be close to Him. Leviticus shows how the Israelites could come close to Him. It took a lot of thought and hard work.

Today, we can come close to God through Jesus. You'll learn a lot more about Him as you read this book!

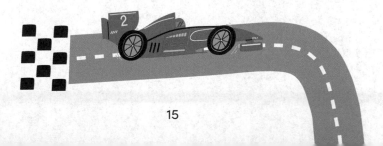

Numbers

Ready. . .

All the people of Israel complained
against Moses and Aaron, and said to them,
"If only we had died in the land of Egypt!
Or if only we had died in this desert!"

NUMBERS 14:2

Set. . .

Trouble happens when we say,
"I won't obey my God today."

Know Your Bible!

It's so easy to complain. But complaining doesn't help anyone. Your mom and dad don't like when you complain, do they? God doesn't like it, either.

You remember, back in Exodus, how God helped His people leave their hard life in Egypt. Now they were on their way to a land called Canaan. It was a beautiful, good place God had promised them. . .and He never lies.

But the people complained on the way. They grumbled. They actually wished they were dead!

It's a very sad story. The people were so disobedient that God gave them what they said they wanted. Because of their complaining, it would take them *40 years* to reach the Promised Land. They would wander in the desert, and all of the complainers would die there. But because God is kind and forgiving, their children would still get to enjoy Canaan.

God is very good. Let's be sure we thank Him, not complain.

17

Deuteronomy

Ready. . .

You will obey all His Laws that I tell you, all the days of your life. And then you will have a longer life. O Israel, you should listen and be careful to do them. Then it will go well with you.

DEUTERONOMY 6:2–3

Set. . .

God gives rules to help us grow,
not because He just says "No!"

Know Your Bible!

Do you enjoy rules? Some people do because then they know what's expected of them. But now or then, almost everyone wants to break the rules. At times we all want our own way.

It's hard to be told, "No!" But sometimes that's the best thing for us. Our parents know it. Our teachers know it. God knows it. . .and God knows everything, so His rules are perfect.

In the book of Deuteronomy, Moses was teaching God's people just before they entered their Promised Land. God had rules for them, and Moses said they should obey. Not because God was taking away their fun. His rules were meant to give people longer, better lives. God wanted things to go well for them, and He knew exactly what would help.

God sets rules for you in the Bible. He'll use your parents or teachers to help you understand those rules. When you know what God wants, just do it. That will make you grow!

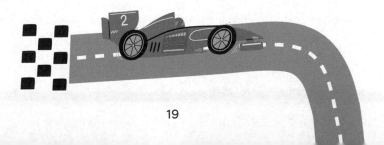

Joshua

Ready. . .

"Be strong and have strength of heart!
Do not be afraid or lose faith. For the Lord
your God is with you anywhere you go."

JOSHUA 1:9

Set. . .

God will make us brave and strong
to do what's right and fight what's wrong.

Know Your Bible!

Joshua was Moses' helper. While Moses led God's people through the desert, Joshua did important things like fighting the people's enemies. He was a good and wise young man.

And God said it would be Joshua, not Moses, who should take the people into the Promised Land. That was a big job, and it made Joshua nervous. So God spoke to Joshua, saying, "Be strong! Don't be afraid! I will be with you wherever you go!"

Have you ever been afraid to do something? Maybe your first day in a new school building made you nervous. Maybe you were given a job you didn't think you could do. But God would say to you what He said to Joshua: "Be strong! Don't be afraid! I will be with you wherever you go!"

Because he trusted God, Joshua did a great job leading the people into Canaan. If you trust God, He'll help you succeed at whatever you need to do too!

Judges

Ready. . .

Then the Lord gave them special
men to judge between what was right
or wrong. These men saved them
from those who robbed them.

JUDGES 2:16

Set. . .

When we're on the devil's track,
God sends friends to help us back.

Know Your Bible!

After years and years of wandering, God's people finally reached the Promised Land. Unfortunately, they forgot that it was God who blessed them and gave them their place to live.

The people walked away from God's plan. They worshipped other gods and broke the rules. The Israelites were troubled by other people who attacked them and stole their things. God was king, though. He gave the Israelites leaders called judges to rescue them.

Sometimes our own sin and mistakes lead us away from God's good plan. We need leaders such as parents, pastors, teachers, and Christian friends to help us find our way back to His right path.

That's what the book of Judges is all about. People mess up. God kindly offers help to make things right. Let's be sure we always follow the (right) leader!

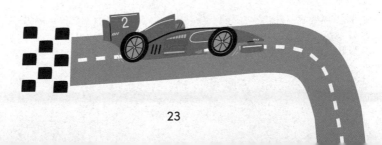

Ruth

Ready. . .

So Naomi returned. And her daughter-in-law Ruth, the Moabite woman, returned with her from the land of Moab. They came to Bethlehem at the beginning of barley gathering time.

RUTH 1:22

Set. . .

When we have faith and loyalty, we become God's family!

Know Your Bible!

Ruth was a woman from a land called Moab. She was not one of God's people, but she married an Israelite man. Sadly, he died—but Ruth knew that her husband's God was the true God. She promised to be loyal to God and to her mother-in-law, Naomi, who was also a widow.

Ruth moved to Bethlehem, Naomi's hometown. She trusted Naomi to teach her the ways of the Israelites. She went out to pick grain in a field so they could have food.

The owner of the field was related to Naomi's husband. Boaz stepped up to help the two women. He even married Ruth! Before long, they had a son, who had a son, who had a son named David. He became king of Israel, and through his family Jesus was born!

God rewarded Ruth for her faithfulness to Him. God will reward your faithfulness too.

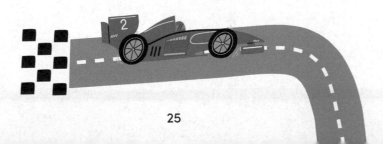

Ready. . .

"But now your rule will not last. The Lord has found a man who is pleasing to him in every way. He has chosen him to rule over his people, because you have not obeyed the Lord."

1 SAMUEL 13:14

Set. . .

Even if you're young and small, God can use you for His call.

Know Your Bible!

Samuel was a prophet and priest of God. He was also the last judge of Israel. When the people begged God for a king like the other nations around them, He told Samuel to find a man named Saul. Then Samuel anointed him—he poured oil over Saul's head to show that this man had been chosen to lead.

For a while, Saul followed God's plan. But then he fell away and disobeyed God. So God told Samuel to find and anoint a shepherd boy named David. He would be the next king of Israel, even though he was the youngest of his brothers. Nobody thought he was important.

But God does things His own way, not always the way anyone else would expect. David was just an unknown shepherd boy. But God saw his heart, and gave David the job of leading His people.

When your heart is clean and full of love for God, He'll give you a special job too. You probably won't rule a nation—but you will do amazing things for Him!

2 Samuel

Ready. . .

So David ruled all of Israel.
He did what was right and good
and fair for all his people.

2 SAMUEL 8:15

Set. . .

David's choices could seem odd,
but in the end he loved his God!

Know Your Bible!

King David really tried to follow God as he led the nation Israel and its army. Unfortunately, like everyone, David sometimes sinned against God. Once, he went so far as to steal a man's wife and have the man killed! But David repented of his sin—he admitted to God how wrong he'd been. Then David accepted the consequences.

God had made a special promise with David to raise up his son Solomon to build a temple in Jerusalem. God said that His love would always be with David's family. Today, we have the privilege of looking back and seeing that God's own Son, Jesus Christ, would be born on earth in David's family line!

The book of 2 Samuel reminds us that following God leads to good things. Our sin may bring us trouble, but God is faithful to forgive us when we ask.

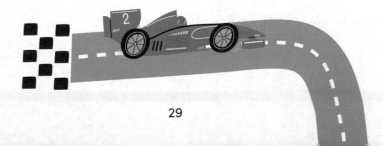

1 Kings

Ready. . .

The Lord said to him, "I have heard your prayer which you have prayed to Me. I have set apart this house you have built by putting My name there forever. My eyes and My heart will be there always."

1 KINGS 9:3

Set. . .

A king who will not guard his heart may see his nation fall apart.

Know Your Bible!

The book of 1 Kings begins with the story of David's son Solomon. As the young, new king, Solomon asked God for wisdom to lead the nation of Israel. God loved this request! He told Solomon that he would receive much wisdom, but also riches and fame.

Over time, though, Solomon wandered away from God. He spent more time constructing his own palace than the temple he was building for the Lord. And he married many women from nations that didn't serve God. Because he wasn't the man that God wanted him to be, his kingdom fell apart when he died. The northern people broke away from the south, and then there were two nations: Israel and Judah. For hundreds of years, they would distrust and fight each other.

Solomon's story shows that wisdom and gifts come from God. But we must be faithful to follow Him completely, and not let ourselves fall into sin. Guard your heart to keep your life from falling apart!

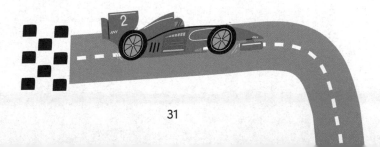

Ready. . .

The angel of the Lord said to Elijah, "Go down with him. Do not be afraid of him." So Elijah got up and went with him to the king.

2 KINGS 1:15

Set. . .

Prophets speak God's word to kings and tell the people, "Do good things!"

Know Your Bible!

The nations of Israel and Judah were made up of God's people. But many of them—and often times their kings—were not following God at all. So He sent prophets to tell the people what He wanted them to know. These stories are found in 2 Kings.

Elijah and Elisha were two prophets who stood up to the bad kings. They told the people about God and what He wanted them to do. The prophets warned Israel and Judah to turn back to God or else they would be invaded by enemy nations. The people kept on sinning, though. In time, the two nations were destroyed by foreign armies.

Today, many people are not following God at all. But you can and should! If you love and serve Jesus, you can be like Elijah and Elisha to your friends and family. Live a good life and tell others how to please God. When you do that, everyone wins.

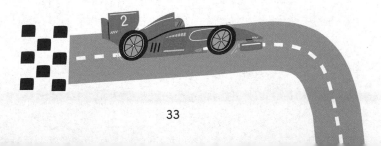

1 Chronicles

Ready. . .

"See, a son will be born to you, who will be a man of peace. I will give him peace from all those who hate him on every side. His name will be Solomon. And I will give peace and quiet to Israel in his days. He will build a house for My name. He will be My son, and I will be his father. I will make his throne in Israel last forever."

1 CHRONICLES 22:9–10

Set. . .

God loved David like a friend
and said his throne would never end.

Know Your Bible!

If you liked the books of 2 Samuel and 1 Kings, you'll like 1 Chronicles. It tells a lot of the same stories!

But this book tells more about David's friendship with God. We see how much work David did getting ready to build a temple for God. The Lord said this place of worship in Jerusalem would be constructed by David's son Solomon.

Solomon followed David as king of Israel, and God promised David that his family line would have a throne that lasted forever. But what does that mean? Israel doesn't have a king today.

The answer to that question includes all of us who aren't Israelites. We know that Jesus came from David's family line—He is the King of all kings. Jesus, our Lord, is the promise that God gave to David!

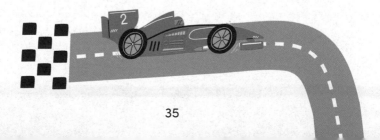

2 Chronicles

Ready. . .

"If My people who are called by My name put away their pride and pray, and look for My face, and turn from their sinful ways, then I will hear from heaven. I will forgive their sin, and will heal their land."

2 CHRONICLES 7:14

Set. . .

When God's people humbly pray,
He forgives and makes a way!

Know Your Bible!

2 Chronicles is a lot like the book of 1 Kings. We read about Solomon's kingship over Israel, then its sad breakdown under his son. When Rehoboam ruled, Israel divided into two kingdoms. The northern one was still called Israel, while the southern kingdom was named Judah.

2 Chronicles pays most attention to Judah. The book was written to remind the people of their history. Judah had a bad habit of following bad kings into sin—but when good kings served God, the nation did well.

Like those old-time Israelites, we need to remember our past. When we think of how bad our disobedience and sin are, we know we don't want to do that again! And when we pray and ask forgiveness, turning away from our sins, God promises to hear from heaven and forgive.

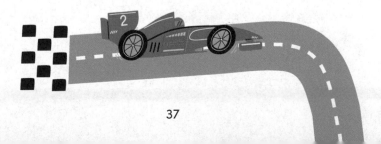

Ezra

Ready. . .

The people of Israel, the religious leaders, the Levites, and the rest of the people who returned from Babylon, set apart this house of God with joy.

EZRA 6:16

Set. . .

God would do what He had planned—return His people to their land.

Know Your Bible!

Ezra was a Jewish priest who led a group of his people back to Jerusalem to rebuild the temple. Many Jews had been carried away as prisoners to Persia. The Persian king, Cyrus, realized God wanted him to release these people. He let them go back to their homeland, and he even gave them back the valuable things an earlier king had taken from God's temple.

After being in a foreign land with foreign gods for so long, these Jewish people needed to re-learn how to worship the one true God. So Ezra taught them. He showed the people that God keeps His promises. God said He would one day bring them back home, and He did.

In the Bible, God has made many promises to us too. He says He'll forgive our sins when we ask. He says He'll always be with us. He says He has a forever home in heaven for us. Knowing that God kept His promise to the Israelites, we can believe He'll keep His promises to us too!

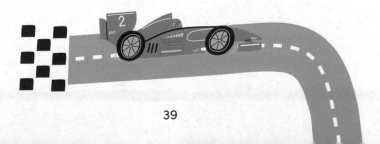

Nehemiah

Ready. . .

"I told them how the hand of my God had brought good to me, and the words that the king had spoken to me. Then they said, 'Let us get up and build.' So they put their hands to the good work."

NEHEMIAH 2:18

Set. . .

See God's people, great and small,
working hard to build the wall.

Know Your Bible!

In the Bible, the book of Nehemiah follows the book of Ezra. And the story of Nehemiah follows right after Ezra's story. Like Ezra had, Nehemiah also traveled out of Persia and back to Jerusalem.

Nehemiah was Jewish, but he had an important job working for the king of Persia. When Nehemiah learned that the walls of Jerusalem were still broken down, many years after enemy armies invaded, he wanted to help. Nehemiah knew that God wanted him to go back to Judah and rebuild the city wall. The king told him to go, and Nehemiah led a project that was done in only fifty-two days!

It's amazing how one man could do so much good for his country. Though you may never have quite as big of a job, your life can still do much good for many people. You may not know exactly what they are yet, but God has big plans for you!

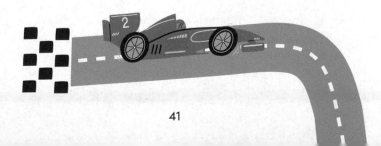

Esther

Ready. . .

"For if you keep quiet at this time, help will come to the Jews from another place. But you and your father's house will be destroyed. Who knows if you have not become queen for such a time as this?"

ESTHER 4:14

Set. . .

Esther was a pretty girl whose boldness truly changed the world.

Know Your Bible!

The book of Esther is like a princess story. We see how a young Jewish girl won a beauty contest to become the queen of Persia.

Esther was an orphan, a child whose parents had died. She had been raised by an older cousin named Mordecai. One day, he refused to bow before the king's most important official. Haman was so angry that he wanted to kill Mordecai—and not only him, but *all* the Jews! Haman got the king to sign a law saying that the Jews would be destroyed. When Mordecai found out, he told Esther that she needed to go see the king. Maybe she could get him to change his mind.

The Persian king had a rule that said anyone who came to him without an invitation could be killed. And Esther did not have the king's permission to visit. But Mordecai told her that she became queen for a moment like this. She bravely approached the king, asking for the Jews to be saved—and the king listened. The Jews were saved, and the evil Haman was killed.

Sometimes it's scary to do the right thing. But God will be with you like He was with Esther.

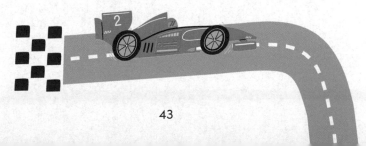

Job

Ready. . .

The Lord said to Satan, "Have you thought about My servant Job? For there is no one like him on the earth. He is without blame, a man who is right and good. He honors God with fear and turns away from sin."

JOB 1:8

Set. . .

Job was good and made God glad.
The jealous devil just got mad.

Know Your Bible!

Job is a story of bad things happening to a good person. Even though Job didn't realize it, his troubles were being caused by Satan. And his life was being protected by God.

The devil wanted Job to quit following God. But because everything—even Satan—is under God's control, he had to ask permission to hurt Job. God said, "Yes."

So Satan brought terrible trouble on Job. He took away the man's children, his wealth, and even his health. Job's friends turned out to be no help, and even his wife told him in Job 2:9 to "curse God and die!" But Job would never do that. Though he didn't understand what was happening—and sometimes he got very frustrated—he kept his trust in God.

The book of Job is a good reminder that when go through hard times, God is still with us. He might allow bad things to happen, but He can use those bad things for our good.

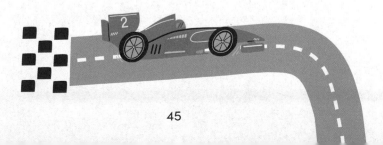

Psalms

Ready. . .

I will give thanks to the Lord with
all my heart. I will tell of all the
great things You have done.

PSALM 9:1

Set. . .

Psalms are songs of joyful praise—
the happy songs to God we raise!

Know Your Bible!

Psalms are songs of ancient Israel, written by several different authors. King David wrote almost half of the 150 psalms. But there were other writers, including Moses.

The psalms are poems about the psalmist's feelings toward God. They are often praise songs about God's glory and love. But some psalms are sad, sharing the writer's hurts and unhappiness with God. Almost every psalm, though, ends on a positive note.

Some psalms were for the Jews to sing as they traveled to Jerusalem. Some were written to celebrate victory over an enemy in battle. Some just beg for God's help and peace in times of trouble. It's easy to find a psalm that relates to your feelings, whether you're happy, sad, or mad.

Did you know that you can be a psalm writer too? When you sing your own song of God's goodness, you are composing a psalm!

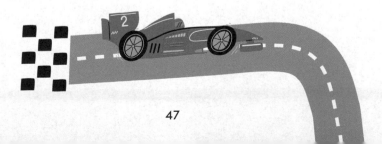

Proverbs

Ready. . .

The fear of the Lord is the
beginning of much learning.
Fools hate wisdom and teaching.

PROVERBS 1:7

Set. . .

In the Proverbs you will find
wisdom for your heart and mind.

Know Your Bible!

Proverbs is a collection of many wise sayings. Several people wrote the proverbs, but the one we think of first is King Solomon. He was the son of David who—when he became king—asked the Lord for wisdom. God answered Solomon's prayer, making him the wisest man on earth!

We can learn much from the proverbs. They teach about living a life that pleases God. One big idea is that knowing God and obeying His Word is what makes us wise and successful. Proverbs also encourages us to learn from our parents, teachers, and elders. They have experienced more in life and have wisdom to pass down to us.

Did you know that Proverbs has thirty-one chapters? Because most months have thirty-one days, many people like to read a chapter each day. That means they'll read the whole book of Proverbs twelves times a year! It's a great way to hide God's Word in your heart and learn to become wiser in life.

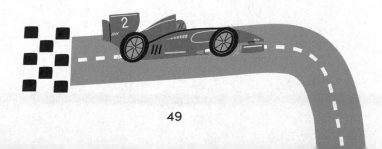

Ecclesiastes

Ready. . .

The last word, after all has been heard,
is: Honor God and obey His Laws. This
is all that every person must do.

ECCLESIASTES 12:13

Set. . .

Life is hard and often sad,
but serving God will make you glad.

Know Your Bible!

The book of Ecclesiastes was probably written by King Solomon near the end of his life. It seems like he was looking back over his life, remembering all the mistakes he'd made. And he felt sorry for the wrong he had done.

Most people want to find the true meaning of life. We wonder if we can really make a difference. In Ecclesiastes, Solomon admits that he chased after his own desires. He wishes he had devoted more of his life to pleasing God and following His commands. That's what will make our lives better too.

Solomon could see that sin and temptation are everywhere. It's easy to make bad choices. But God is everywhere too. He gives us His Word and Holy Spirit to keep us from making poor decisions in life. God wants the best for you, so do what He says. This is all that every person must do.

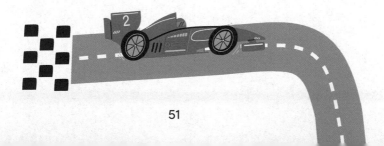

Song of Solomon

Ready. . .

Many waters cannot put out love.
Rivers cannot cover it. If a man were
to give all the riches of his house
for love, it would all be hated.

SONG OF SOLOMON 8:7

Set. . .

God made marriage and its joys
for when we're grown-up girls and boys.

Know Your Bible!

Many people think Solomon wrote this love poem for his wife. Other people think someone else wrote it in honor of Solomon. Either way, the "Song of Solomon" is all about how strongly the king and his bride feel for each other.

God made marriage to be a special relationship between a man and a woman. When we're grown up and want to get married, we honor God by choosing someone who loves and serves Him. Good marriages are a picture to the world of God's love for His people.

Until we're old enough to be married, let's work at being good friends, shining the light of God's love to others. Caring, giving, and forgiving will help us to be good husbands and wives when the time comes!

Isaiah

Ready. . .

"See, God saves me. I will trust and not be afraid. For the Lord God is my strength and song. And He has become the One Who saves me."

ISAIAH 12:2

Set. . .

Isaiah told of Jesus brave—
God's Messiah, sent to save.

Know Your Bible!

The prophet Isaiah wrote this book during a time when his nation was disobedient to God. The Lord told Isaiah to warn the people of Judah that if they did not turn from their sin, they would be carried away as prisoners.

But the book of Isaiah isn't just for those people who lived in Judah so many years ago—it's for us too! This book shows how God was offering salvation to His people if they would just turn away from their sins. Today, He offers salvation to *us* when we turn to Jesus!

The books of Matthew, Mark, Luke, and John (you'll read about them on pages 88–95) are called "the four Gospels"—books that tell the good news about Jesus. Some people call Isaiah "the fifth Gospel," because it told so much about Jesus long before He was born in Bethlehem. Only God can tell the future like that. And only Jesus offers us a perfect future with God.

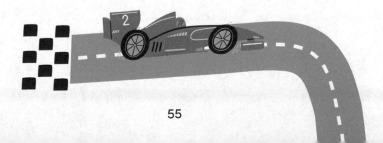

Jeremiah

Ready. . .

" 'For I know the plans I have for you,' says the Lord, 'plans for well-being and not for trouble, to give you a future and a hope.' "

JEREMIAH 29:11

Set. . .

God is wise and has a plan
for His woman and His man.

Know Your Bible!

God gave Jeremiah a special job—he was going to speak for God to the nations. Jeremiah couldn't believe it. He was just a kid! But God said He had planned this job for Jeremiah even before he was born.

The words Jeremiah spoke were tough for the people to hear. The young prophet told about the judgment God was going to bring on sinful people. But those words were very important. Jeremiah trusted God and shared His message, no matter how other people responded.

Do you ever feel like you're too young or unimportant to serve God? Don't believe it! God chooses people for His special jobs, and then He provides the strength to do them. He has a plan. Trust Him to work out His plan in your life.

Lamentations

Ready. . .

The Lord is good to those who wait
for Him, to the one who looks for Him.

LAMENTATIONS 3:25

Set. . .

When life is hard and we are sad,
God gives hope to make us glad.

Know Your Bible!

To "lament" is to be very sad and to cry out in your sadness. The writer of Lamentations—many people think it was the prophet Jeremiah—was crying out in his sadness after the nation of Judah was invaded by Babylon. God used Babylon's king and army to punish Judah for their many sins. . .sins they just wouldn't give up. The people were carried away as prisoners.

Most of Lamentations is very, very sad. But right in the middle of the book, in chapter 3, Jeremiah turned to God with hope in his heart. He knew that God gives peace even in our sadness. He trusted God's promises that the people of Judah would one day return to their homes.

Think of a time when you were very sad about something. Maybe someone you know was sick, or you'd lost something special, or your feelings had been hurt. But then imagine Jesus standing right beside you, putting His arm around your shoulders and telling you everything will be all right. That's what He does for everyone who follows Him. The Lord is good!

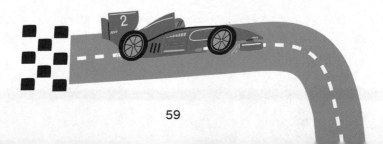

Ezekiel

Ready. . .

"I will give them one heart, and put a new spirit within them. I will take the heart of stone out of their flesh and give them a heart of flesh."

EZEKIEL 11:19

Set. . .

When we pray and do our part, God will really change our heart!

Know Your Bible!

The book of Ezekiel was written by a prophet named (you guessed it!) Ezekiel. While he was living in Babylon with the other Jews carried away from their homeland, he wrote down what God told him to say.

Ezekiel told God's people that even though they were being punished for their sins, they should still turn back to Him. If they would leave their sins behind, they could still be restored to their homes. God never *wanted* to punish His people, but their continuing sin forced Him to act. But Ezekiel reminded them of God's salvation and deliverance.

God called Ezekiel a "watchman," someone who stands guard and warns the people of coming trouble. We can be watchmen too! Let's remind ourselves and our friends to make good choices. When we're tempted to lie or cheat or disobey our parents, let's say "No! I will not disobey." If you have welcomed Jesus into your life, you have a new heart that can obey God every time.

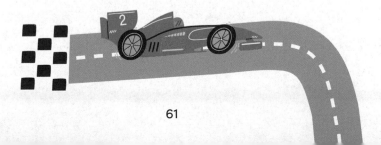

Daniel

Ready. . .

"My God sent His angel and shut the lions' mouths. They have not hurt me, because He knows that I am not guilty, and because I have done nothing wrong to you, O king."

DANIEL 6:22

Set. . .

You're safe with God no matter when— like Daniel in the lion's den.

Know Your Bible!

Daniel was a young Israelite taken from his home by the enemy Babylonians. Even from a young age, though, he and his friends were faithful to God. They refused to eat the food their new boss, the Babylonian king, offered them. Instead, they ate fruits and vegetables. Because they obeyed God, they were the healthiest young men in the king's service!

God made Daniel very important in Babylon. Several different kings trusted him for his wise advice. Other people in the king's court, though, were jealous of Daniel. Do you know the story of the men who tricked King Darius into throwing Daniel into a pit of hungry lions? Happily, God closed the mouths of the lions and Daniel was safe.

At times in your life, some people will dislike you and try to get you in trouble. No matter what, stay faithful to God. He will help you through every hard thing you face. Be like Daniel—God will never let you down!

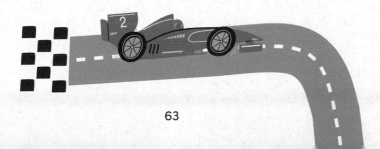

Hosea

Ready. . .

"Those who were not loved, I will call,
'My loved ones.' Those who were not
My people, I will call, 'My people.' And
they will say, 'You are my God!'"

HOSEA 2:23

Set. . .

Even when we disobey,
God loves and wants us back to stay.

Know Your Bible!

God gave the prophet Hosea a hard assignment. To teach His people how much He loved them, God told Hosea to marry a woman who would not love him back. Though Hosea treated her well, she ran away to other men. This was a picture of the way God's people in Israel and Judah treated Him.

God wanted a beautiful relationship with His people, but they kept running away from Him. They followed other gods and sinned against the one true God who loved them very much. After a time, Hosea even had to buy his wife back from a slave market. Many years later, God would buy His people back, from their slavery to sin. The price was the death of Jesus on the cross.

The "happy ending" to Hosea's story is the way God loves His people. No matter how wrong we are, no matter how often we sin, He will welcome us back. Just admit you're wrong and say you're sorry. He will call you, "My child!"

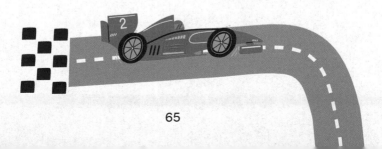

Joel

Ready...

"I will pay you back for the years that your food was eaten by the flying locust, the jumping locust, the destroying locust, and the chewing locust, My large army which I sent among you."

JOEL 2:25

Set...

Locusts eating everything
help to show us God is king.

Know Your Bible!

Joel was a prophet in Judah before the nation was destroyed by Babylon. He knew that God is patient and loving. He knew that God gives His people many more chances than they deserve.

But, like any good parent, God sometimes disciplines His children for doing the wrong thing. So He sent millions and millions of locusts—hungry bugs like grasshoppers—to eat Judah's crops. God also dried up the rain for a while, and let fires burn the fields.

Joel told the people that they needed to admit their sins and turn back to God. If they did that, He would restore their land and provide plenty of food. God is that kind and generous.

God still disciplines His children. He will use hard times to get our attention when we're doing the wrong things. Like the ancient Israelites, we have the chance to admit our sins and turn back to Him. When we do, we'll find forgiveness, hope, and happiness.

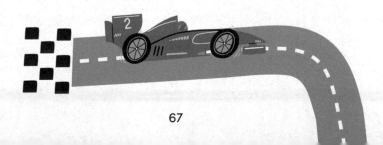

Amos

Ready. . .

"But let what is fair roll down like waters. Let what is right and good flow forever like a river."

AMOS 5:24

Set. . .

Amos had God's Word to share: "Do what's right and good and fair."

Know Your Bible!

Amos wasn't a king or a priest or anyone "important"—he was just a shepherd who God chose to speak to the people of Israel. They worshipped false gods. They took advantage of other people. They didn't love what God loves: caring for others, being kind, and doing right.

The Israelites were making lots of money, but their hearts were evil. They even took money from those who had little! And they didn't want to hear the truth.

So God told Amos to warn the people. Even though everything seemed to be going right, they were headed for trouble. Over and over God gave His people a chance to make things right. But they chose to follow their own ways.

Don't be like those people Amos preached to! Ask God to help you be fair and good and right. And when you make a mistake, ask Him to forgive you. He will.

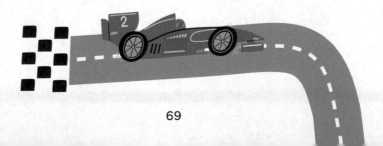

Obadiah

Ready. . .

"For the day of the Lord is near for
all nations. As you have done, it will
be done to you. What you do will come
back to you on your own head."

OBADIAH 15

Set. . .

Never laugh when others fall.
God will not be pleased at all.

Know Your Bible!

Obadiah is a bit of a mystery. We don't know much about the man who wrote the shortest book in the Old Testament. We do know he spoke God's words against a foreign nation rather than God's people in Israel or Judah.

This prophecy was against the nation of Edom. The Edomites were related to God's people because they came from Isaac's son, Esau. Esau's twin brother, Jacob, was the founding father of Israel. There were bad feelings between these nations for hundreds and hundreds and hundreds of years.

When the people of Israel were escaping from their slavery in Egypt, Edom did not help them. They would laugh when Israel was disciplined by God. Obadiah warned Edom that the Israelites were God's chosen people. Edom was not and would be destroyed for good.

Never laugh or gloat when others fail. Jesus taught that we should love even our enemies. God wants us to be kind and helpful to everyone—maybe someday, those enemies could even become friends.

Jonah

Ready. . .

When God saw what they did, and that
they turned from their sinful way, He
changed His mind about the trouble
He said He would bring upon them,
and He did not destroy Nineveh.

JONAH 3:10

Set. . .

Jonah had a job to do
and God would help him see it through.

Know Your Bible!

Jonah tried his best to run away from the job God had given him to do. The Lord wanted Jonah to preach to Nineveh, capital of the evil nation of Assyria. Jonah knew how wicked the Assyrians were, and he did *not* want to share God's word with them.

So Jonah climbed aboard a boat going in the opposite direction. But God wasn't going to let Jonah get away that easily. He sent a storm to stop Jonah's escape! The runaway prophet was tossed overboard and swallowed by a giant fish. For three hot, smelly, awful days in that fish, Jonah thought and prayed. He decided he would obey God after all.

God made the fish spit Jonah onto the shore. From there, he found his way to Nineveh and told them God would destroy them if they didn't repent. To Jonah's surprise, they did repent! They were sorry for what that they had done wrong and asked God to forgive them.

Like Jonah, we Christians have a job from God. He wants us to be a light to our world, helping people to see what they're doing wrong and how to make things right. And, like Jonah, we can be sure that when God gives us a job, He will help us do it.

73

Micah

Ready. . .

O man, He has told you what is good.
What does the Lord ask of you but to
do what is fair and to love kindness, and
to walk without pride with your God?

MICAH 6:8

Set. . .

People who are on God's side
are kind and fair and without pride.

Know Your Bible!

Micah was a prophet at the same time as Isaiah, Amos, and Hosea. Seems like God really wanted to get His message across!

Micah told the people of Israel and Judah that trouble was coming because their leaders did not obey God. The Lord wanted these leaders to set a good example of caring for others.

But they were selfish, and it seemed like everyone was taking advantage of each other—especially of the poor. Micah warned those who were doing wrong to change their ways. What God wanted wasn't hard to understand. His people should do what is fair, love kindness, and live without pride before Him.

Like most prophets, Micah had some really bad news. But he also had some very good news—in fact, the best news of all. Micah predicted that a special ruler would be born in Bethlehem, someone who would one day make everything right. We know that ruler is Jesus!

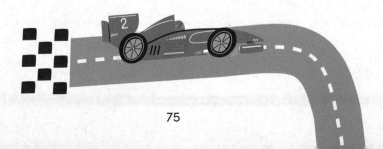

Nahum

Ready. . .

The Lord is good, a safe place
in times of trouble. And He knows
those who come to Him to be safe.

NAHUM 1:7

Set. . .

When you're in a troubled place,
God is safe and full of grace.

Know Your Bible!

When you read the book of Nahum, you'll notice a name you've seen before: *Nineveh*. Do you remember that God wanted Jonah to preach there? The people in that capital city of Assyria obeyed God for a while after Jonah's prophecy. But then they fell back into their old sinful ways.

Nahum came with the same message Jonah had preached a hundred years earlier. He said Assyria would be destroyed for its wrongdoing. Assyria's soldiers were making life hard for God's people, the Israelites. Because of this, they would face destruction.

God was using Assyria to discipline to His own people, the Israelites. But He was still unhappy with Assyria's sin. So God told Nahum to warn the Assyrians, while offering hope to the Israelites. Anyone who turns to Him will find that He is good and safe!

Habakkuk

Ready. . .

As for the proud one, his soul is not right in him. But the one who is right and good will live by his faith.

HABAKKUK 2:4

Set. . .

God's good plan will come about.
Let's have faith and never doubt.

Know Your Bible!

Most of the time, God "talks" to us through His Word, the Bible. We don't usually hear Him speaking out loud.

But the prophet Habakkuk did, and he wrote down those conversations in a short book of the Old Testament. Habakkuk had many questions to ask God. He especially wondered why sinful people got away with doing bad things.

In response, God said He knew what was happening in the world. And He was going to make everything right. Habakkuk just needed to be patient.

God's message to Habakkuk was the same as His message to us today. We need to trust Him, believing by faith even when we don't understand. Don't worry—God's got everything under control.

Zephaniah

Ready. . .

The Lord your God is with you, a Powerful One Who wins the battle. He will have much joy over you. With His love He will give you new life. He will have joy over you with loud singing.

ZEPHANIAH 3:17

Set. . .

God is love! He'll even sing when you take Him as your king.

Know Your Bible!

Zephaniah grew up under two of Judah's worst kings, Manasseh and Amon. They sinned by worshipping false gods and performing sacrifices to them. But Zephaniah served the one true God. He warned his nation about following wicked kings and serving fake gods.

Most of this short book talks about punishment for sin. But it ends with a beautiful picture of a coming day when God makes Israel healthy and good. He will be so pleased that He'll rejoice over His people with singing!

You don't have to wait until the end of time to enjoy God's love. Right now, He rejoices when you believe in His Son, Jesus Christ. That makes you a member of God's family. He becomes your Father and you become His much-loved child.

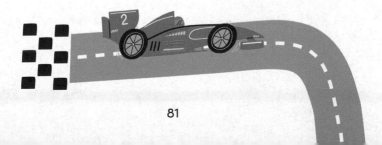

Haggai

Ready. . .

So the Lord moved the spirit of Zerubbabel. . .ruler of Judah, and the spirit of Joshua. . .the head religious leader, and the spirit of all the rest of the people. And they came and worked on the house of the Lord of All, their God.

HAGGAI 1:14

Set. . .

Back at home, the time is when the temple must be built again.

Know Your Bible!

Haggai was a prophet who urged the people of Judah to do a job: rebuild God's temple. The people had been prisoners in Babylon, but now they had returned home to Jerusalem. Led by Ezra and Nehemiah, they had worked to rebuild their city—but they spent more time building their own homes than God's house.

So God sent Haggai to fire up the people. And they actually listened to him! They began to rebuild the temple and put away their sin. Many prophets had warned the people before, and they didn't care. Haggai got to see obedience, and God promised to bless them.

When you know what God wants from you, do it right away. Don't ever waste time in doing right. Obey, with the strength God gives you. He'll be happy, you'll be blessed, and the world will be better off!

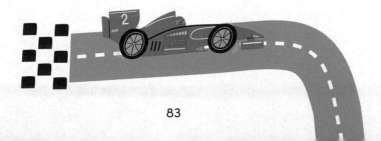

Zechariah

Ready. . .

Then he said to me, "This is the Word of the Lord. . . 'Not by strength nor by power, but by My Spirit,' says the Lord of All."

ZECHARIAH 4:6

Set. . .

We can only do what's right
by the power of God's might.

Know Your Bible!

Zechariah was an Israelite born in Babylon. He grew up to be a prophet and priest, and was one of the first Jews to return to Jerusalem after their "exile." That's a word that means the people were forced to live away from their real home.

Zechariah and Haggai preached around the same time. But while Haggai wanted God's people to rebuild the temple, Zechariah wanted them to look far into the future. He reminded the people of the promised Savior, a King who would one day ride into Jerusalem on a donkey. Many hundreds of years later, we know that King was Jesus.

And Zechariah told about things even farther into the future—at the very end of time. Guess what? Jesus is there too! By His power, He will make the world peaceful and perfect. He will be King over everything.

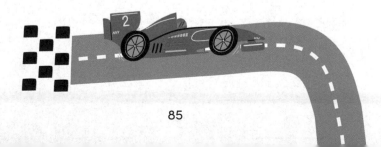

Malachi

Ready. . .

"But for you who fear My name, the sun of what is right and good will rise with healing in its wings."

MALACHI 4:2

Set. . .

Follow God with all your heart.
Never give Him just a part.

Know Your Bible!

Malachi wrote the last book of the Old Testament. He prophesied in Judah about a hundred years after the people returned from exile. They had rebuilt their temple, but they didn't really understand who God wanted them to be.

The Lord spoke through Malachi to remind the people of His love. Because He loved them, He wanted them to be better than they were. The people had become careless and lazy in the way they worshipped God.

As always, God gave them a chance to change their ways. And for those who respected and trusted Him, there would be good days to come. In fact, a great day was coming when "the sun of what is right and good" would rise to heal people from their sin. That "sun" would be Jesus!

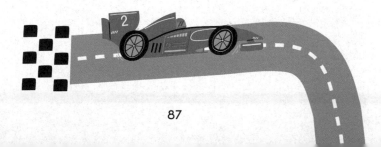

Matthew

Ready. . .

"For sure, I tell you, unless you have a change of heart and become like a little child, you will not get into the holy nation of heaven."

MATTHEW 18:3

Set. . .

Jesus loves a childlike soul.
He saves and heals and makes it whole.

Know Your Bible!

Matthew is the first book of the New Testament, the part of the Bible that tells about Jesus' life and death and teaching. Matthew was a follower of Jesus. He wanted to show his fellow Jews that the Old Testament prophets had said Jesus would come. And now He was here!

It had been hundreds of years since the last prophet, Malachi, spoke for God. Then John the Baptist appeared, saying that Jesus was the Messiah, God's special leader. Matthew explained that Jesus was the Savior the people had been waiting for.

At the end of the book of Matthew, we find the "Great Commission," Jesus' job for His followers. He said, "Go and make followers of all the nations. Baptize them in the name of the Father and of the Son and of the Holy Spirit" (Matthew 28:19). Jesus' disciples started doing that almost two thousand years ago. Today, we should do the same, helping everyone we know to meet Jesus too.

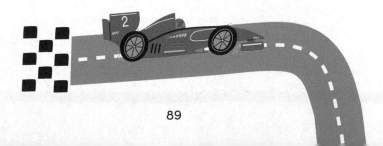

Mark

Ready...

"For the Son of Man did not come to be cared for. He came to care for others. He came to give His life so that many could be bought by His blood and be made free from sin."

MARK 10:45

Set...

Jesus came to earth to serve.
That's so much more than we deserve!

Know Your Bible!

Jesus is king of the whole world. But the book of Mark shows that He came as a servant. Jesus, who is God, made Himself less so people could be saved from their sin.

Mark shows many miracles that Jesus did. He came to earth to help people, making the sick well, helping the blind to see. But ever more than that, He wanted to heal their souls and give them a way to heaven.

Jesus showed incredible kindness when He died on the cross. That's when He took the punishment for everybody's sin. Anybody who believes in Him can be made free from their sin, saved to life that lasts forever.

Have you received Jesus as your Savior? If so, great. If not, you can pray this prayer: "Jesus, I believe You are Lord over all. Your death paid the price for my sins. Please forgive my sins and make me part of Your family. Thank You!"

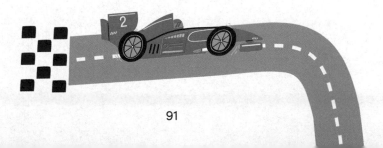

Luke

Ready. . .

"Which of these three do you think was a
neighbor to the man who was beaten by the
robbers?" The man who knew the Law said,
"The one who showed loving-pity on him."
Then Jesus said, "Go and do the same."

LUKE 10:36–37

Set. . .

Do every bit of good you can,
like the good Samaritan.

Know Your Bible!

Luke tells many of the same stories as Matthew, Mark, and John. But this third "Gospel"—a book that tells the story of Jesus' life—is the only one to mention the "good Samaritan."

Jesus told about a man who was robbed and beaten as he traveled from Jerusalem to Jericho. He was left on the side of the road, almost dead. A couple of religious leaders, men who are supposed to know and follow God, passed by the man without helping him. The person who did stop to help was from a place called Samaria. The Samaritans were not friends of the Jews, so it seems strange this man would help an enemy.

Jesus used this story to teach His disciples (including us today) to show God's love to everyone. Can you think of someone who needs to know Jesus? How can you show God's kindness to that person today?

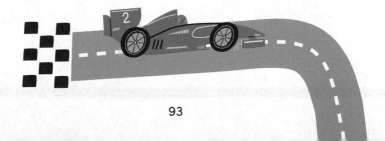

John

Ready. . .

"For God so loved the world that He gave His only Son. Whoever puts his trust in God's Son will not be lost but will have life that lasts forever."

JOHN 3:16

Set. . .

Life that never, ever ends—
Jesus gives to all His friends.

Know Your Bible!

The disciple who wrote the book of John is known as "the disciple Jesus loved." What a nickname! John was Jesus' closest friend on earth—but by believing in Him, *anyone* can be Jesus' friend today.

John wrote about several miracles of Jesus, including raising a man named Lazarus from the dead. But the greatest miracle of all is being "born again." Jesus told a Jewish leader named Nicodemus that he needed to be born again to become a child of God. Nicodemus was confused. How could an old man like him get back inside his mother's belly?

Jesus, though, was speaking of a spiritual birth. We must come to know Him by His Spirit, being "born again" in the Spirit to have our sins forgiven. Jesus is the only way to heaven and life that lasts forever. Believe Him for yourself, and make sure you tell others about Him!

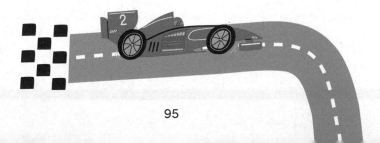

Acts

Ready. . .

When they heard these words, they said nothing more. They thanked God, saying, "Then God has given life also to the people who are not Jews. They have this new life by being sorry for their sins and turning from them."

ACTS 11:18

Set. . .

The book of Acts has happy news: salvation is for more than Jews!

Know Your Bible!

The book of Acts is sometimes called "The Acts of the Apostles." The apostles were the twelve men Jesus chose to follow Him, then go out into the world to tell His story. In Acts, we learn about the people who believed their message and began the Christian church.

Those first Christians shared the Gospel—the good news of Jesus—everywhere they went. They told people who were Jews like themselves, but they also shared Jesus with Gentiles.

A Gentile is anyone who is not Jewish. God made the Jews His special people, so they could show His goodness to the whole world. They often sinned and made God angry—but it was through the Jewish people that Jesus was born. And through Jesus, *anyone* can be saved. It doesn't matter if you're a Jew or a Gentile, as long as you believe in Him.

The book of Acts shows how God started to send the message of Jesus to the whole world. Aren't you glad that message was shared with you?

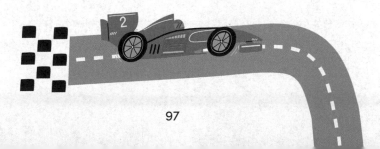

Romans

Ready. . .

I am not ashamed of the Good News. It is the power of God. It is the way He saves men from the punishment of their sins if they put their trust in Him. It is for the Jew first and for all other people also.

ROMANS 1:16

Set. . .

Through Jesus we are saved from sin and made completely new within.

Know Your Bible!

Romans is the first book in the New Testament written by the apostle Paul. But we first meet Paul in the book of Acts. Then, he was a Jewish religious leader known as Saul. Saul had been making life very hard for the Christians. But then he met Jesus on the road to Damascus and was completely changed! Soon, he was called Paul and became a missionary.

Paul wrote this letter to the church in Rome. Romans is a very important book that explains sin and salvation. Paul said very clearly that all of us are born with sin in our hearts. We all need Jesus' salvation to defeat our sin nature and make us new.

After we believe in Jesus, Paul says we have peace with God. We are no longer enemies but friends. Even better than that, we become God's children! And we can look forward to a day when He will make us perfect, taking us home to live forever with Him.

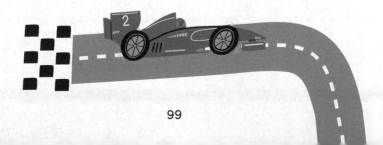

1 Corinthians

Ready. . .

And now we have these three:
faith and hope and love, but
the greatest of these is love.

1 CORINTHIANS 13:13

Set. . .

Faith and hope and love are blessed,
but always know that love is best.

Know Your Bible!

Corinth was an important city in the apostle Paul's day. It had a Christian church, but the people in that church had problems. They were arguing and taking each other to court. They couldn't agree on much of anything. So Paul wrote them a letter, telling them not to live in sin like the people who didn't know Jesus.

The Corinthians really needed to learn about love. So Paul taught them what love really looks like. It is patient and kind and forgiving. It is not angry or prideful or jealous. Love is against sin and for God's truth. Real love makes everything better.

It was God's love that sent Jesus to die for our sins so that anyone who believes in Him could have life that lasts forever. It is our love for others that makes them want to learn about Jesus. This week, look for ways to show love to others. They'll be pleased, you'll be pleased, and God will be pleased!

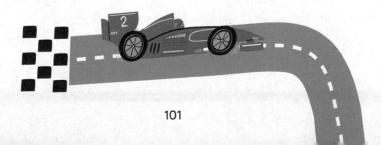

2 Corinthians

Ready. . .

We do not look at the things that can be seen. We look at the things that cannot be seen. The things that can be seen will come to an end. But the things that cannot be seen will last forever.

2 CORINTHIANS 4:18

Set. . .

The new has come, the old is gone—
in Christ our lives go on and on.

Know Your Bible!

The second letter to Corinth is a bit different than the first. The Corinthian Christians had made some changes to their attitudes and actions, and the apostle Paul called them "dear friends."

Paul wrote this letter to remind the people that their trust and hope was in Jesus Christ. When they believed in Jesus, they became totally new people. Their old lives were over with. Now there was no reason to be afraid of death. On earth, our bodies get old and die. But Christians can look forward to a brand-new body that will never, ever die. God has promised this, and we believe it by faith.

Since God has been so good, the Corinthians (and all of us as Christians) should turn away from every sin. We honor God when we give every bit of ourselves to Him.

Galatians

Ready. . .

Even so, we know we cannot become right with God by obeying the Law. A man is made right with God by putting his trust in Jesus Christ. For that reason, we have put our trust in Jesus Christ also. We have been made right with God because of our faith in Christ and not by obeying the Law.

GALATIANS 2:16

Set. . .

The rules will never save your soul.
Trusting Jesus is the goal.

Know Your Bible!

Galatia wasn't a city but a region, a large area with several churches. The apostle Paul wanted these Galatian Christians to stop trying to please God by following the rules of the old Jewish Law. Instead, they should focus on the goodness of Jesus and the freedom He offered.

Paul wanted the Galatians to enjoy the blessing of being sons and daughters of God. That's what they became when they put their trust in Jesus! They should still honor God by the things they said and way they acted. But they didn't need to follow all the rules of the Old Testament.

As Christians, having God's Holy Spirit in our lives, we can grow the "fruit" of love, joy, peace, not giving up, being kind, being good, having faith, being gentle, and being the boss over our own desires. There's never been a law against those things!

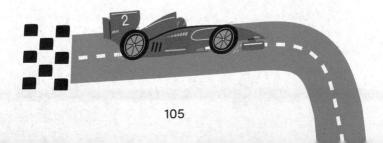

Ephesians

Ready. . .

Do as God would do. Much-loved children
want to do as their fathers do.

EPHESIANS 5:1

Set. . .

You can know your life is great
if God's the one you imitate!

Know Your Bible!

Ephesus was another important city in the apostle Paul's time. It had a big, beautiful temple to a false goddess called Diana. But Paul preached about the true God and His Son, Jesus, and many people became believers. Toward the end of his life, Paul wrote this letter to the church to help them become stronger, more mature believers.

Paul reminded the Ephesians that God had chosen them to be His children. He wanted them to be holy and without sin. Though Jesus' sacrifice on the cross, the Ephesians (and all of us today) could be saved from sin, filled with God's Spirit, and made better every day. They would keep moving forward in their Christian lives if they just acted like God by loving others, staying away from sin, and living in the light of the truth.

All of those things will lead us to happiness. And then we should give thanks to God for the great things He does!

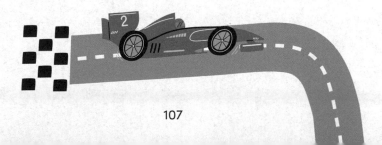

Philippians

Ready. . .

Do not worry. Learn to pray about everything. Give thanks to God as you ask Him for what you need.

PHILIPPIANS 4:6

Set. . .

In Philippians you read
God gives everything we need.

Know Your Bible!

This letter to Christians in Philippi was written while Paul was in prison! But even though he was going through hard things, his love for Jesus and other people gave him much joy.

The book of Philippians is full of joy and thankfulness. The hardships that Paul faced were bringing glory to God. Everyone in his prison knew he was there because he served Jesus, and even the guards were hearing how to be saved. Other Christians saw these things and became braver in telling people about Jesus. That made Paul happy.

The great apostle wrote that he'd learned life is all about Jesus, and death means having even more of Jesus. Because of that, we should never worry. We can pray and ask God for everything we need. Then we can thank Him for everything He gives!

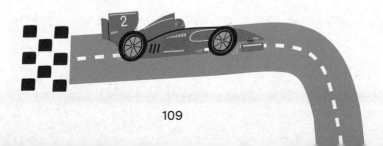

Colossians

Ready. . .

Christ is our life. When He comes again, you will also be with Him to share His shining-greatness.

COLOSSIANS 3:4

Set. . .

Jesus is our life, it's true!
Because He saved us, we are new.

Know Your Bible!

The book of Colossians reminds us that *Jesus is God*. The apostle Paul wrote to the church in Colossae to fight a false teaching that made Jesus less important. Paul reminded the people that Jesus is the most important leader in the whole universe!

Jesus is the only way to salvation, eternal life in heaven with God the Father. But Jesus also gives us new life now, in this world. Our life in Christ looks much different from our old, sinful lives. It's like we take off the bad things we used to do—such as lying, cheating, and disobeying our parents—and we put on our new "clothing" of holiness. Holiness is being close to Jesus and letting Him lead us in all that we should do.

With this new outfit, we look more and more like Jesus. We are able to be patient, to show kindness to others, to love and forgive. How is your life different since Jesus saved you?

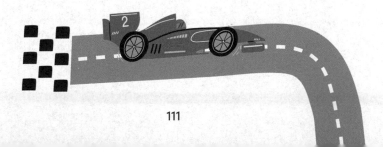

1 Thessalonians

Ready. . .

The Lord Himself will come down from
heaven with a loud call. . . . First, those
who belong to Christ will come out of
their graves to meet the Lord. Then,
those of us who are still living here on
earth will be gathered together with
them in the clouds. We will meet the Lord
in the sky and be with Him forever.

1 THESSALONIANS 4:16–17

Set. . .

Live for Jesus, stay in prayer,
until we meet Him in the air.

Know Your Bible!

The apostle Paul had started the church in Thessalonica, and he loved it very much. Paul had introduced these people to Jesus. Now he wanted to explain what would happen when Jesus came back to earth.

To be ready for that day, the people needed to live holy lives, set apart for service to God. Paul encouraged the Thessalonians to watch for Jesus' return. They should be aware of what was going on in the world. They should not fall into the bad behaviors and sins of those who don't believe in God. Jesus will come back without warning, so Paul wanted every Christian to be ready.

At the end of his letter, Paul urged the Thessalonians, "Be full of joy all the time. Never stop praying. In everything give thanks (1 Thessalonians 5:16–18)." Sounds like a great way to get ready for Jesus, doesn't it?

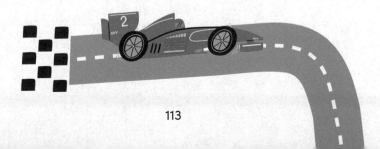

2 Thessalonians

Ready. . .

Our Lord Jesus Christ and God our Father loves us. Through His loving-favor He gives us comfort and hope that lasts forever. May He give your hearts comfort and strength to say and do every good thing.

2 THESSALONIANS 2:16–17

Set. . .

Always do the things you should.
God is pleased when you do good.

Know Your Bible!

Paul wrote a second letter to the Thessalonians shortly after the first. Someone told the church members that Jesus had already come back, and the people were upset. So Paul made sure they knew that Jesus' second coming was still in the future. They shouldn't believe everything they heard.

Until Jesus did return, Paul said, the believers of Thessalonica should work hard and do right. This honors God! For kids today, Paul's words might mean you clean your room when your parents ask. Or you help in the nursery at church. Or you mow some elderly neighbors' grass or bake them cookies.

Never get tired of doing good. Living out your faith, every day, is the mark of a true child of God!

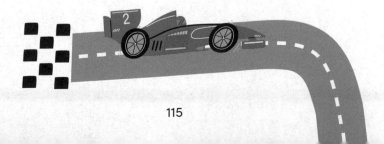

1 Timothy

Ready...

Let no one show little respect for you because you are young. Show other Christians how to live by your life. They should be able to follow you in the way you talk and in what you do. Show them how to live in faith and in love and in holy living.

1 TIMOTHY 4:12

Set...

Even if you're not that old,
your faith can be mature and bold.

Know Your Bible!

An older pastor, the apostle Paul, wrote this letter to a younger pastor named Timothy. Paul loved Timothy. In fact, he called Timothy "my son in the Christian faith."

Paul gave advice to Timothy to help him lead his church. The apostle wrote that church leaders should be well-respected, good spouses, and good parents. They shouldn't chase after money or drink. Their first desire should be to serve God with a holy life.

And any Christian can live this way. Paul told young Timothy that nobody should disrespect him because of his age. He should live such a good life that others would see God in him.

This is great advice for you too!

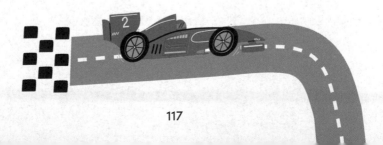

2 Timothy

Ready. . .

I have fought a good fight.
I have finished the work I was
to do. I have kept the faith.

2 TIMOTHY 4:7

Set. . .

Being Christian can be hard,
but heaven is a great reward.

Know Your Bible!

The book of 2 Timothy may be the last letter the apostle Paul wrote. Most people believe Paul was martyred—that means he was killed for serving Jesus. But before he died, he wanted Timothy to know that God is faithful, even in the hard times.

Paul wrote that Christians will face a lot of hard times. Sometimes we'll even suffer because we believe in Jesus. But Paul reminded Timothy (and all of us) to hold on to the truth, to stay faithful to God.

Hard times can make us wonder if God is still with us. But we know from the Bible that God is *always* with us. He will never leave us on our own. And even when our final day comes, guess what? We close our eyes on earth and open them in heaven, where we'll be with God forever.

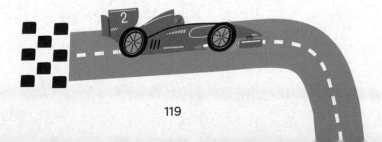

Titus

Ready. . .

But God, the One Who saves, showed how kind He was and how He loved us by saving us from the punishment of sin. It was not because we worked to be right with God. It was because of His loving-kindness that He washed our sins away.

TITUS 3:4–5

Set. . .

Paul taught something very true: we're not saved by the good we do.

Know Your Bible!

Along with 1 and 2 Timothy, Titus is a "pastoral letter." Titus was another young church leader who the apostle Paul called a "son in the faith."

Titus led a church on an island—Crete, in the Mediterranean Sea. Paul wanted Titus to watch out for false teachers who tried to change the Word of God. Like he did with Timothy, Paul gave advice on how to choose and train other church leaders. It was so important that Titus and his fellow workers held firm to the truth of the Bible and set a good example for others.

But Paul reminded Titus that doing good things didn't save him—only faith in Jesus gives us life that lasts forever. But when we really know Jesus, we are able to do the things that make Him happy. We are not saved *by* our good works, but *to do* good works!

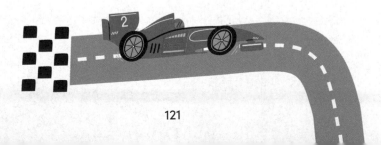

Philemon

Ready. . .

Do not think of him any longer as
a servant you own. He is more than
that to you. He is a much-loved
Christian brother to you and to me.

PHILEMON 16

Set. . .

Forgiving love is Jesus' way.
We should do that every day!

Know Your Bible!

The "book" of Philemon is only one chapter long! It is the shortest of the apostle Paul's letters, and it was written to one man about something personal. Paul was asking Philemon to forgive a former slave.

The slave, named Onesimus, had run away from Philemon. But Onesimus had somehow met Paul in prison and become a Christian. Paul wanted Philemon to take Onesimus back, not as a slave but as a Christian brother. Paul even said he would pay any bills that Onesimus owed.

The book of Philemon is an important reminder that forgiveness is the key to our faith in Jesus. We are to forgive other people as He forgave us—completely, without holding grudges. Is there anyone you need to forgive today? Ask Jesus to help you forgive and love as He does.

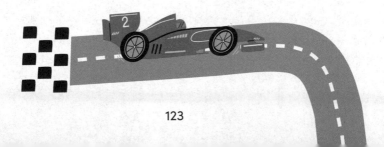

Hebrews

Ready. . .

Now faith is being sure we will get what we hope for. It is being sure of what we cannot see.

HEBREWS 11:1

Set. . .

Faith is trust that God is true
and knowing Jesus makes us new.

Know Your Bible!

We don't know who wrote the book of Hebrews. But we know this book teaches many important things about faith. Hebrews was written to show Jewish Christians that Jesus' way is so much better than the old rules of the Law.

During Old Testament times, God's people had to follow strict rules about what to eat, how to wash, and when to work. There were ten big commandments, and hundreds of little ones. If the people messed up, they had to bring an animal to the temple for a sacrifice.

The book of Hebrews proves that Jesus met all of God's demands perfectly. He died on the cross as the greatest sacrifice of all time—a sacrifice that never needs to be made again. Now, when we believe in Him, we can have a relationship with God that doesn't require all of those old rules.

We believe all of these things by faith, our deep trust in what God has said and done. This is what pleases Him most!

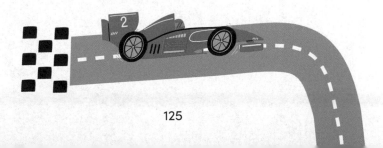

James

Ready. . .

A man becomes right with God by
what he does and not by faith only.

JAMES 2:24

Set. . .

Our faith is shown by good we do.
How we live proves if we're true!

Know Your Bible!

The book of James was probably written by a half-brother of Jesus. His mother, Mary, had four other boys, named James, Jude, Joseph, and Simon. If it's the same James, he became a believer after Jesus' resurrection and then an important leader in the early church.

James might be the very first New Testament book to be written. It gives advice on living the Christian life. We can show others the truth of our faith by the good things that we do. James wrote, "A faith that does not do things is a dead faith" (James 2:17).

Does your life show your faith in Jesus Christ? Does the way you talk let people know that you are a Christian? Do you have a reputation for doing the right thing? All of these things prove to others that you love and follow Jesus.

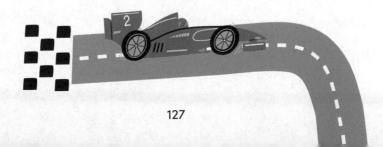

1 Peter

Ready. . .

Show respect to all men. Love the
Christians. Honor God with love and fear.
Respect the head leader of the country.

1 PETER 2:17

Set. . .

In persecution or in need,
show respect for all who lead.

Know Your Bible!

One of Jesus' closest disciples, Peter, wrote this letter to both Jewish and Gentile Christians. Peter wanted them to honor God with their lives even when they were laughed at and hurt for being Christians. That is called "persecution."

It would have been very hard for Peter's first readers to respect and pray for their leaders. The Roman government was led by a wicked man who put Christians in prison and even killed them. Peter knew it wouldn't be easy, but living a life that honors God means honoring *all* people with His love.

Sometimes it's hard to respect our leaders. But Peter's words are for all of us. Let's honor all people with the love of Jesus. You never know when your kindness and respect might lead them to accept Jesus too.

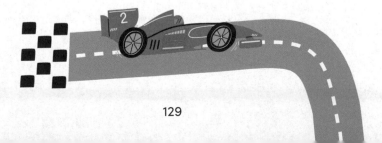

Ready. . .

The Lord is not slow about keeping His promise as some people think. He is waiting for you. The Lord does not want any person to be punished forever. He wants all people to be sorry for their sins and turn from them.

2 PETER 3:9

Set. . .

Though it seems it's taking long, God will one day right all wrong.

Know Your Bible!

Peter wrote his second letter to Christians everywhere. He wanted them to know what it meant to live a holy life. We must remember that the Bible wasn't made up by men, but is the actual word of God! Peter knew that false teachers were trying to confuse the followers of Jesus. So he encouraged Christians to beware of anyone who would lead them away from the truth.

Peter finished this letter by describing the way the world will end. When God knows the time is right, He will destroy this world with fire! But Peter was careful to say that God is not in a hurry to do that. He wants everyone to be saved, so He gives people lots of time to turn to Him. Some people laugh at God's patience, but we know that "the long waiting of our Lord is part of His plan to save men from the punishment of sin" (2 Peter 3:15). Then He will remake the world to be perfect forever. How good God is!

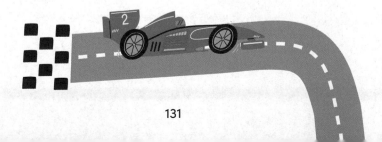

1 John

Ready. . .

We love Him because He loved us first.

1 JOHN 4:19

Set. . .

It's really true, without a doubt—
love is what God's all about.

Know Your Bible!

John wrote a very encouraging letter to all believers. He wanted us to know how to live a holy life and avoid false teaching. John wrote a lot about love.

Because John knew Jesus personally (he was even called "the disciple Jesus loved"), he is a great person to teach us these truths. John reminded his readers that Jesus came to earth as a man. Because Jesus lived a perfect life without sin, paid the price of sin on the cross, and then rose again from the dead, He could make us right with God. The Father forgives our sins through the Son, whenever we ask.

This is an amazing picture of love! God knew exactly what we needed, and He sent Jesus to earth to provide it. The salvation that Jesus offers makes us God's children, and He becomes our Father. This is all possible because God *is* love (1 John 4:8).

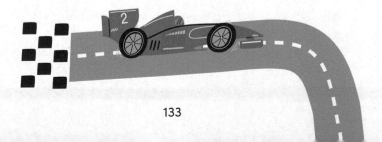

2 John

Ready. . .

There are many false teachers in the world. They do not say that Jesus Christ came in a human body. Such a person does not tell the truth. He is the false-christ.

2 JOHN 7

Set. . .

We know Jesus Christ is real,
the Son of God who came to heal.

Know Your Bible!

John wrote his second letter to a family. He was warning them about false teachers.

Some people were saying that Jesus had not come to earth as a man. But John knew that wasn't true—he had seen and heard and even touched Jesus when He was on earth. So John warned about anyone who says anything about Jesus that doesn't match the apostles' teaching.

John's message is important for us today too. Some people say the Bible isn't God's Word, or that Jesus isn't really God. Some false teachers say Jesus isn't the only way to heaven.

But our salvation depends on Jesus being exactly who He says He is. He called Himself "the Way and the Truth and the Life" (John 14:6), and we believe Him. John knew these things because he spent three years walking and talking with Jesus. We read John's letters, and believe in Jesus by faith!

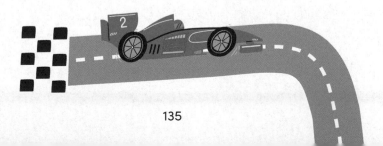

3 John

Ready. . .

Dear friend, you are doing a good
work by being kind to the Christians,
and for sure, to the strangers.

3 JOHN 5

Set. . .

Ways we honor God include
the sharing of our home and food.

Know Your Bible!

Has your family ever hosted a dinner party or welcomed someone to stay at your house? This is called hospitality. And the book of 3 John is all about that.

John's third letter shows the difference between two men. Diotrephes did not offer hospitality to God's people, while Demetrius was known for doing the right thing. Would you rather be known for your kind service or for kicking people out of the church? That's an easy choice, isn't it?

Ask your mom or dad if you can offer hospitality like Demetrius. Maybe you could invite a family from church to have dinner at your house. Or maybe you could take a meal to an older person who can't get out. There are many ways to show hospitality—and they all please God.

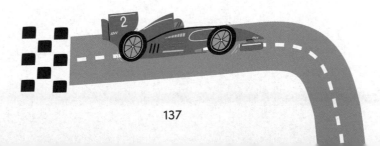

Jude

Ready. . .

Dear friends, you must become strong
in your most holy faith. Let the Holy
Spirit lead you as you pray.

JUDE 20

Set. . .

In our faith we must be strong
so we don't end up doing wrong.

Know Your Bible!

Like the writer of James, Jude was another half-brother of Jesus. Jude's short letter encourages believers to stand up against false teachers and fight for their faith. Jude wanted people to understand how dangerous it is to let false teachers lead us away from the truth of Jesus.

While Jude urged us to be strong in our faith, he also wanted us to show gentle love to people who do not yet believe. But we must never let non-Christians pull us into sin. Jude reminded his readers that only God can keep us strong: "There is One Who can keep you from falling and can bring you before Himself free from all sin" (Jude 24).

When we know God through Jesus, His Holy Spirit gives us the strength to do the right thing. We can build up our "faith muscles" as we study the Bible and pray, and keep ourselves in God's love. There's no better place to be!

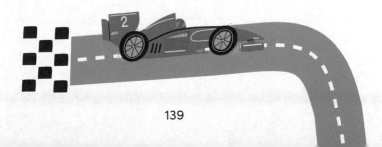

Revelation

Ready. . .

I heard a loud voice coming from heaven. It said, "See! God's home is with men. He will live with them. They will be His people. God Himself will be with them. He will be their God."

REVELATION 21:3

Set. . .

Sin and sadness pass away
when Jesus comes to save the day!

Know Your Bible!

God gave John an incredible vision of the end of this world and the coming of the new heaven and new earth. The book of Revelation does contain scary scenes of judgment and death. But as Christians, we see hope in this book.

All of the sin, sickness, and suffering of our world will one day pass away. God Himself will wipe away all of our tears! We will worship Him forever in a perfect place.

That is all possible because Jesus will come like an army commander, wiping out Satan and all the enemies of the Lord. If we have accepted Jesus as savior, we are God's friends. We can look forward to being on the winning side!

When you go through hard times in your life, remember that God says He will change everything for the good. And that day is coming soon.

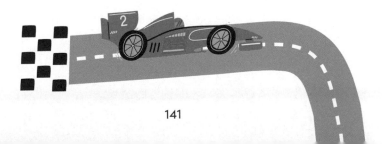

Another Great Devotional for Kids!

Boys and girls, ages 5 to 8, will be engaged and encouraged as they learn timeless truths from God's Word! Every reading in this delightful devotional will challenge kids to run their faith race with strength and perseverance, as they're prompted to get *Ready, Set,* and *Pray!* with each turn of the page.

Paperback / 978-1-64352-861-8 / $7.99